WASHINGTON, D.C.

CLB 1782
© 1989 Colour Library Books Ltd, Godalming, Surrey, England
Printed and bound in Hong Kong by Leefung-Asco Printers Ltd
All rights reserved
Published 1989 by Arch Cape Press, distributed by Crown Publishers, Inc.
ISBN 0 517 63114 8
h g f e d c b a

© 1989 Colour Library Books Ltd, Godalming, Surrey, England
Printed and bound in Hong Kong by Leefung-Asco Printers Ltd
All rights reserved
Published 1989 by Arch Cape Press, distributed by Crown Publishers, Inc.
ISBN 0 517 63114 8
h g f e d c b a

WASHINGTON, D.C.

Text by
BILL HARRIS

ARCH CAPE PRESS
New York

People who live out in the northwest corner of the United States forever feel obliged, when they travel, to make it clear that they live in Washington State and not the District of Columbia. It's not that they have anything against the capital of their country. It's just that most Americans think of Washington, D.C. as a place to visit and are usually impressed to think they've met someone who actually lives there. Most people don't seem to think anybody lives there, and they are always amazed to find out that it is home to 626,000 people. This is in spite of the fact that every two years someone spends a lot of time and money trying to convince them that there is nobody better qualified to watch out for their interests in the House of Representatives, and, parenthetically, to live in Washington, D.C. Senators do the same thing every six years, and, of course, presidential candidates every four. In every case, one of the things they get for their trouble is to go to Washington to live, at least for a while.

Their constituents continue to visit them at the rate of nearly 18 million a year. They spend about $1.5 billion each year, some of it in the fourth largest concentration of hotel rooms in the world, which makes tourism the District's second-biggest employment category. Anyone who visits there knows who the biggest employer is. Even people who don't work directly for the government work at something that wouldn't exist if the government wasn't there.

Until they finally gave up in the late 19th century, the city's business community worked long and hard to attract industry to the Washington area, and for very good geographical reasons. But it was a losing battle and nobody tries any more. In fact, the local Convention and Visitors Association points with pride to the fact that "the absence of heavy industry has made Washington one of the cleanest cities in America."

It is also one of the most beautiful of the world capitals, and one of the few that never really intended to be anything else. And it was a nice place to live even before it became the Federal City in 1790. At least that's what the people who were there said when they were asked to sell their land and move.

But they themselves had worked hard to convince their neighbor, George Washington, that the capital city ought to be located at the base of the Cumberland Mountains, where they could socialize with lawmakers in an atmosphere far,

far away from the bustling industrial north. President Washington was agreeable. After all, it was less than a day's ride from home in countryside he dearly loved. But, politics being what it is, he bided his time waiting for the right moment to make his wishes known. Meanwhile there were others making their wishes known all over the place. Very good proposals came from cities as far apart as Kingston, New York and Annapolis, Maryland. The State of Virginia even offered its old capital at Williamsburg lock, stock and barrel, and said it would sweeten the deal with cash to spruce it up.

But at that point it was a foregone conclusion that Philadelphia would get the honor. It was where the whole thing began, and most members of the Continental Congress had gotten used to the place. When the War of Independence was over, they went back to the City of Brotherly Love almost by habit. They hadn't realized that the people they represented would do the same thing. In the summer of 1783 it came home to them with a vengeance in the form of 300 war veterans who marched on the city in search of what they called "leadership." What they were really looking for was back pay, and they expected Congress to listen to them. When they set up camp in front of the State House, Congressmen looked out the windows and complained that the authority of the United States was being insulted, and called on the State of Pennsylvania to call out the militia (it's unclear who was supposed to pay them). When the governor refused, they did what other Congresses would be accused of doing in future generations: they walked away from the problem. They went all the way to Princeton, New Jersey, in fact.

When the first snows began to fly, they fled again to the more hospitable climate of Annapolis, Maryland, and then went back north in the spring to Trenton, New Jersey. They moved on to New York after that, and it was there that the new president got them all to agree to move their operation to the banks of the Potomac. After the smoke cleared, they also agreed to go back where they came from. Presumably the war veterans had broken camp by then, and Philadelphia became the capital city again during the ten years it took to get the new Federal City habitable.

It's amazing they could have done it in ten years. Once Congress agreed on the site in 1790, the Maryland Legislature voted to give the Federal Government nearly seven square miles. Virginia followed them quickly with another three, but there was very little money to do anything more than build a Capitol, a President's Palace and a Navy Yard. And the planters who were already settled there expected to be paid for their houses and farms. The president appointed three respected local men to reason with them, but after a year of friendly persuasion, the negotiations were still going nowhere. Washington himself finally met with them during an evening of drinking and good comradeship among old neighbors at a Georgetown tavern. The next morning most of them remembered that they had agreed to accept slightly more than $66 an acre for their land if it were to be used for buildings, but nothing at all for the land needed for streets and avenues.

It seemed like a fair deal. And the wine had been good and the company pleasant. But in the cold light of day the planters began noticing a little man with surveyor's instruments cutting across their fields. He had been there for more than a month, but nobody had taken him too seriously. He was obviously trying to decide where the streets would go, but until they realized that they were donating the land for that part of the city, they hadn't cared much about what he was doing as long as he didn't get in the way of their fox hunts.

Now they saw him in a different light and began speculating among themselves about this man, Major Pierre Charles L'Enfant. He had been a hero in the late war, and he had designed the elegant building in New York that Congress had recently abandoned. "But he's from Paris," some said, "and the Champs Elysee is one of the widest boulevards in the world. Suppose he likes that sort of thing." Others pointed out that the Major's father had been a gardener at Versailles. "What if he wants to bring those Frenchy ideas of big gardens and lush parks here?" they asked. The gossip went on for weeks as the French engineer crisscrossed their estates with an enigmatic smile on his face. They finally agreed to end the speculation by asking President Washington back to Georgetown for some more wine and some more conversation. It was a sobering evening for all of them. The city plan he showed them covered 6,611 acres, but only 541 of them would be used for public buildings. More than 3,600 acres was to be used up by streets and avenues. But before they could object too much, the president pulled an ace from his sleeve. Add 3,600 to 541 and the total is only 4,141. That left 2,470 acres that weren't needed by the new Federal City and could be sold as commercial property. The only catch was that the government, as formal title-holder of the whole tract, would keep half the proceeds of any sale, with the other half going to the original owner. Since they all knew that those left-over parcels would be worth hundreds of dollars more than the $66 they had already agreed to, they signed on the dotted line and the site of the Federal City became federal property on the last day of June in 1791.

L'Enfant had been turning the plans over in his mind for almost three years by then. He had asked for the job before anybody knew there would ever be a need for such a plan. But though he had finally become the personal choice of President Washington, himself a former surveyor, and had been hired by Secretary of State Thomas Jefferson, an important architect, nobody bothered to tell him what they'd like to see in their new city. That was fine with L'Enfant, who wasn't too keen about supervision anyway, and who considered himself one of the great artists of his day. He may well have been, but among the qualifications for the job, the art of politics was far and away the most important. In the months that followed, a lot of people called him a lot of things, but no one ever accused him of having a flair for politics.

He submitted his first formal plan for the new city in August, 1791. By then both Jefferson and Washington had given him their ideas, the president suggesting discreetly that perhaps they didn't need so many wide avenues, and Jefferson saying that a wide mall might be nice. Jefferson also suggested that the streets should be numbered alphabetically east and west from the Capitol and numerically north and south. L'Enfant followed their suggestions, but the bulk of the plan was entirely his. It was different from, and better than, any other city on the face of the earth. He included the traditional grid pattern, but broke its monotony with radial roads that not only created plazas and views, but used existing roads, which should have impressed the landowners as much as the fact that he eliminated some avenues and shortened others.

It took a lot more than that to impress them. But L'Enfant never took a single step in that direction. When it came time to hold the first auction of the commercial parcels, nobody had a copy of the plan to show potential buyers. The engineer said he had sent it to Philadelphia, where an engraver was still fooling around with it. When they asked him for another copy, he sent their messengers back empty-handed. L'Enfant had never made it a secret that he was opposed to selling commercial property in his city, and when the first sale fell flat, the blame fell squarely on the Frenchman's shoulders.

His troubles were just beginning. New Jersey Avenue existed on his plan as a straight line from the Naval Yard to the Capitol. But along the right of way, Daniel Carroll, kinsman of the most influential people in Maryland, and one of the most important of all the local landowners, had begun to build a manor house for himself. Work had started before the site of the city had been determined, and the foundations were about six feet into the planned right of way. Carroll said L'Enfant had agreed to make the avenue a bit narrower. L'Enfant said he had never agreed to any such thing and ordered his construction crew to tear the house down. The president agreed to pay the outraged landowner for his loss. The engineer refused even to apologize. "It would have afforded a dangerous precedent," he said.

Then, as if to prove how dangerous precedent could be, when a second auction of commercial property was announced, he sent his maps to the same Philadelphia engraver as before, and the same thing happened again. Once again the auction had to be held without a map to let buyers know what they were bidding on. In February 1792, one month short of a year from the day he started the job, Major Pierre Charles L'Enfant was fired. But he never left town for long, and for the next 20 years he walked the streets of the new city, passing silent judgement on the ways his plans were altered, but obviously proud of how slight the alterations were. Of all the people who have made their mark on Washington, D.C., a city where politics and compromise are usually all that matters, the most lasting impression was made by this man who would rather have died than compromise or have anything to do with politics.

Once the government moved into its new city, everyone seemed to lose interest in it. Roads were left unpaved, construction, except on the Capitol and a few other important buildings, almost stopped. And there were stories of workmanship having been so poor that when the city was attacked during the War of 1812, a lot of public servants who felt that serving in the nation's capital was about the same as a hardship post on the wild frontier thought seriously of helping the British soldiers torch the public buildings.

After the Civil War, other cities began making proposals to move the capital. They said that now that the country was moving west, the center of its government should do the same. What they meant was that the District of Columbia had become such a terrible place to live that they were convinced good people were shunning high office. The Mall extended out from the Capitol, as the original plan had intended, but at the other end were slaughterhouses and squatters' shacks. There were still swamps and marshes within a short mosquito flight of the White House. And most of the grandly-conceived avenues were still dirt roads.

Things began to take a turn for the better when one Alexander Shepherd was elected president of the common council in 1862. Not many of the old Washingtonians liked him very much and, though he kept agitating to improve the city, they were able to hold him at bay. Then, in 1868, Ulysses Simpson Grant moved into the White House. Shepherd and Grant were soul-mates, and the two men spent long hours sipping whiskey at the Willard Hotel. What they talked about was the city outside the hotel's doors and what might be done to make it a better place to live.

In 1871, Congress changed the status of the local government and the man in charge was to be a territorial governor appointed by the president, who was also given the power to appoint some other local officials. Because Shepherd had irritated the members of Washington's Oldest Inhabitant's Society, Grant was smart enough not to make him governor. But he did appoint a Shepherd crony and gave his friend an important spot on the board of public works. Shepherd's first act was to propose a four million dollar bond issue for civic improvements. His second was to begin work on streets and sidewalks before the money was raised. The community leaders filed an injunction against the bonds, and he countered by stopping construction on the spot. Even dirt roads had been better than torn-up roads, and when a special election was held to make the bonds legal, people sick of all that mud on their shoes overwhelmingly passed it.

Shepherd was almost unmerciful in his campaign for civic betterment after that. A railroad track that ran down Maryland Avenue vanished in a single night. More than a thousand questionable buildings vanished almost as quickly. Pennsylvania Avenue was paved for the first time, and nearly 120 miles of other streets and avenues got the same treatment. Canals were filled in, new waterpipes installed, sewers were finally connected to hundreds of houses for the first time, and no less than 50,000 street trees were planted. By the end of his first year, Shepherd had spent the four million he raised in the bond issue and had saddled the District of Columbia with a staggering debt of nearly $9.5 million. The taxpayers were appalled. Even though they had a better city for it. They took their case to Congress, which responded by holding an investigation. In the end it was revealed that the District's debt was more like $18 million and the bills were still coming in. Congress responded by doing away with the government it had created in favor of a commission. Needless to say, Mr. Shepherd was not one of the commissioners. When last seen he had a train ticket to Mexico in his hand.

But he left behind a city that had bought some pride, even if the price was high. There were new buildings going up, new parks being created and houses had a new look of permanence. He hadn't done much to the Mall except cooperate with a railroad company in building a massive Gothic terminal about where the National Gallery is today. The tracks cut across the Mall itself, which made life a little difficult for strollers. But there weren't many of those in the 1870s; the Mall seemed to be reserved for cows and sheep and chickens. Meanwhile, Shepherd had left another legacy for Washingtonians. With the abolition of the territorial government, Congress took away their right to vote for their own local officials in exchange for guarantees that the city would never be bankrupt again. For the first time, the Washington Establishment settled down to the fact that the District would be the capital of the country and nothing more. The boosters who had been dreaming of attracting industry put their dreams away and began to think of other ways to make their fortunes. There were four universities in the District by then, the Library of Congress was already the most important in the country, and the newly-built Smithsonian Institution joined with them to give a touch of culture and scholarship to the place. Such things can be good for real estate values.

Washington became a publishing center at about the same time. The Government Printing Office provided more tonnage than most of the established firms in Boston and New York, and as the capital of the country, it was a terrific place to put out a newspaper or publish a magazine. Most of the other light industry that had crept in crept out again. When the C&O Canal stopped operating in the 1890s, nobody seemed to care.

About the only industry to survive the new disinterest was the brewing business, which by some accounts tripled in the last years of the old century.

Washington had begun thinking about its centennial when James McMillen, a new man in the Senate from the State of Michigan, introduced a bill to improve the city's park system. Congress had already developed the site of the National Zoo, about a mile out of town, and had begun building a park along the banks of Rock Creek leading up to it from the Potomac. The long-delayed landscaping of the Capitol grounds had been completed by Frederick Law Olmsted thirty years before, but the greensward between the Capitol and the river was still a disaster area.

In 1893, the Columbian Exposition in Chicago had begun an enthusiasm among Americans called the "city beautiful" movement. The great architects of the day had created a gleaming "White City" on the shores of Lake Michigan where a short time before there had been a swamp. Every city in the country became convinced it could do the same, and waterfronts from Boston to Charleston, Chicago to Cleveland, became focal points for a new breed of city planners who decreed that the natural environment was a natural complement to heroic architecture. Senator McMillen had been infected by their enthusiasm and had little trouble passing it on to his colleagues.

It was a grand plan. In essence, it was L'Enfant's plan. An idea whose time had finally come. The so-called McMillen Plan, unveiled in 1902, was a blueprint for orderly growth, and an answer to the incursions that had been imposed on the original scheme in the preceding hundred years. The Library of Congress and the Treasury Department, among other important buildings, had been placed at odds with L'Enfant's symmetry, and the Washington Monument, which had stood as an ugly stump due to lack of funds for nearly 30 years, was hopelessly off center. But the Commission was pleased that enough of the original plan had been left untouched to make their ideas work.

The plan called for orderly placement of public buildings, with museums joining the Smithsonian along the Mall. Buildings related to the legislative branch would surround the Capitol, and those connected with the judicial would have the Supreme Court for a neighbor. The Mall itself would get a memorial to President Lincoln, separated from the Washington

Monument by reflecting pools. It all seems obvious to those of us who have enjoyed the plan's results, but in 1902 it was a dramatic proposal.

There were some snags, of course. One of the biggest was the fact that, while McMillen's committee was planning fountains and gardens and recreation areas for the Mall, the Pennsylvania Railroad had secured Congressional approval to expand the railroad station and put more tracks between the Capitol and the Washington Monument. The planners were forced to follow the railroad's president across Europe before finally getting a formal audience that resulted in an agreement to build a Union Station, with Congress footing most of the bill.

The cost of the station was a drop in the bucket compared to the overall projected cost of the beautification of the District of Columbia. Americans were used to big numbers coming out of Washington by then, but when they were told that it would cost about $600 million to spruce up their capital, a lot of eyebrows were raised. Chief among them were on the faces of members of the House of Representatives, who had felt left out of the discussion when Senator McMillen formed his commission without asking them for advice. The Senator died that summer and it looked very much like the plan would die with him. The architect Charles Follen McKim, and Daniel Burnham, the Chicago architect who had served as the Commission's chairman, took up the cudgel. They had served on the commission for a year without compensation, and were certainly looking for a return on their investment. But beyond that, along with the others, the "city beautiful" movement had become an obsession with them. Their lobbying was eventually successful, and in the first decade of the 20th century a dozen or more impressive buildings, including Burnham's Union Station and office buildings for the House and Senate, were unveiled. The prevailing architectural style was the same Classical form that marked the Capitol itself and had impressed everyone who saw the Beaux Arts Columbian Exposition less than 20 years before.

But though vistas are an important part of Classical design, little was done about the parks that had been the stated purpose of the McMillen Commission in the first place. In response, Congress created a new body, the Fine Arts Commission, in 1910. Members of the House who still pretended that the Senate-created Parks Commission didn't exist were happy at last.

From that day forward, it became impossible to build a monument or place a statue without Arts Commission approval. The architects and artists among the commissioners made some enemies in the process, but few of them were members of Congress. And as they began to implement the McMillen plan by planting flowers and trees everywhere, property owners were quick to get on the bandwagon and improve their own front yards. Those who didn't get the feeling were finally brought into the mainstream of beautiful thoughts when the mayor of Tokyo made a gift of 2,000 cherry trees to Mrs. William Howard Taft. She had them planted around the Tidal Basin and every citizen of the District of Columbia gasped when they all bloomed at the same time in the spring of 1915.

Parts of the plan never did see the light of day. There were waterfalls and sunken gardens lost by the wayside, and a planned esplanade along the river became a highway instead. But in spite of an occasional wart, the plan resulted in a "city beautiful" that is the pride of a nation.

Work on making the plan a reality went on long after all the men who started the ball rolling had died. Some of the work of the Fine Arts Commission was handed over to the National Capital Park and Planning Commission, formed in 1926. They were able to cut the red tape and get work moving on the new Supreme Court Building, designed by Cass Gilbert, who had made a name for himself with the Woolworth Building in New York. When the Court moved into its new home in 1937, the new National Archives building was keeping the moving men busy at the same time.

If official Washington was getting spiffy, many of the residential parts of town were still neglected. But except for the very poor, most Washingtonians felt a burst of pride when the Washington Star bragged in a 1909 editorial that their city would teach every other city in the country "... cleanliness of mind and honesty and the municipal faith." And that it would show them "the soul of the beauty that lies within and the beauty that shines without." And why shouldn't they be pleased? When the heat and the humidity got to them in midsummer, they could go down to the Tidal Basin and take a dip in the same water that froze in the winter and made a dandy ice-skating rink, not to mention a place to meet that special someone. The trolley line had been extended all the way out to the zoo, and many who had originally objected to having it so far out of town, where it seemed to be virtually the private property of people with horses and bicycles, were pleased to be able to make the lions and tigers and bears the object of a day's outing. The city had its own professional baseball team by then, and the young men of the town had dozens of new fields to play the game themselves. And everyone was rightly proud of the democracy of the place. It was possible for a shopkeeper to meet an ambassador on the tennis court and for a shopgirl to meet a titled European out for a stroll, and even have him offer to row her in a small boat on the river. Or during the years when Teddy Roosevelt, at least, was in the White House, it was possible for a youngster to play "king of the hill" in Rock Creek Park with the children of the president. Or even with the president himself.

During those years between beautification and World War I, the structure that made some people matter more than others in the District of Columbia began to totter and to change. Up until then, there had been an organization known as the Oldest Inhabitants Association that kept close tabs on who was who. People in government, largely, didn't count because anyone with any sense could tell they were from someplace else and as soon as they were found out they were going back there. During Washington's first hundred years, the old inhabitants made a fair living off the people who came to serve in Congress or in other Federal departments, but almost never socialized with them. Very few public servants, even those who served there all their lives, bought property in the city, which was one of the criteria for social status. It was customary for lawmakers to live in boardinghouses or hotels, or at the very least to rent furnished houses. Of the 25 presidents elected before the turn of the century, 12 had lived in rented space in Washington before moving into the White House. Seven of them had never lived in Washington at all before their election.

It was after the District made its place in the city beautiful movement that it suddenly became a tourist attraction. Americans had visited their capital before, but usually in the spirit of the 300 war veterans who marched on Philadelphia looking for their back pay. After the 20th century began, those visits became pilgrimages, very nearly a religious experience for many. And visitors from abroad could usually count on finding the real face of America in its capital. Americans went there from every corner of the country, even the State of Washington. They still

do, and the experience is just as breathtaking to today's citizens, who have seen the Capitol dome and the grounds of the White House almost every day on their television screens.

By the time William Howard Taft moved into the White House in 1909, the social structure of the city had changed completely, and the "in-crowd" was determined by the voters rather than by a "we were here first" fiat. It was ironic that the society that was pushed aside was denied the right to vote for the man they thought would make the most engaging neighbor over at 1600 Pennsylvania Avenue. Washingtonians didn't get that right until 1961.

Many members of Washington's old established society simply retreated into their shells and pretended it didn't matter that the parties were getting to be more glittery, and more expensive, with each passing year. By and large, the people the voters sent to become their neighbors brought well-heeled hangers-on with them, or in many cases were well-heeled themselves and were used to using their money to create an impression. Some old-timers said they enjoyed the fact that they didn't have to set the pace for society any more and that they finally had the chance to choose whether they'd play the game at all. But the desire to be on the inside is a basic human emotion and in the capital of the United States it was a fine art. Those who didn't participate, whether by choice or not, became known all over town as "cave-dwellers." And everyone knew that it was only a matter of time before the Oldest Inhabitants would be as extinct as the cave man. The children of many of the old families began seeking their fortunes elsewhere or threw in their lot with the Federal officialdom, which itself was expanding at an almost alarming rate. By the 1920s the only way to be an important fish in the Washington pond was to get yourself elected, or be close to someone who had.

But even if social status was finally granted after the turn of the century to politicians that Washingtonians once regarded as carpetbaggers, the government was becoming something more than a collection of statesmen concerned with governing a growing country. New bureaus were bringing scientists and social researchers into the District of Columbia. For the first time the city was firmly on course toward becoming the cultural center residents had longed for a half century earlier. The museums and galleries were bursting at the seams and talking seriously of expansion. Theaters were hanging Standing

Room Only signs from their marquees, and someone even organized a local symphony orchestra, which played to packed houses for one season in 1902. After it disbanded, visiting orchestras filled the void, and by the time the Wilson administration settled in, no one in Washington felt starved for intellectual stimulation.

Washington had been attacked during the War of 1812 and had become an armed camp during the Civil War, but the city had never known quite the same uneasiness that settled in when the president invited the German ambassador to go home in 1917. People who didn't know what might happen next kept a close eye on people they thought did know. The jitters took hold when Congress established an agency for National Defense and various agencies around town put armed guards at their gates. The tension lasted, and built, for more than two months until the president asked Congress for a declaration of war. Within days the quality of life in the city of Washington took a dramatic turn. It would never again be a sleepy southern town.

The District of Columbia became the nerve center of the war effort. New agencies were created and staffed with newcomers to the city. The military installations nearby were expanded, bringing thousands more into the area. Embassies of allied countries expanded and uniforms of every description became fashionable among strollers on the Mall. The population of the city doubled in a year, and for the first time Washington, D.C. took its place as a world capital. Important businessmen from every part of the country began spending more time there. Educators and scientists took up residence there. Temporary buildings were constructed on the Mall to house the new agencies. Their staffs were left to their own devices to find a place to live. Many homeowners took in boarders for the first time, and eventually Congress agreed to spend money to build dormitories for homeless government workers.

When the war finally ended, a lot of the new residents packed their bags and went home again, as had happened after other wars. But in 1918, the bulk of the people who had come to do their bit for the war effort seem to have decided to stay. The temporary office buildings and the dormitories stayed, too. The city became, in the view of old-timers, an impersonal place where you could take a long walk on a Sunday morning and never see a familiar face. It had become a boom town.

With the boom came automobiles. And with automobiles, traffic jams, parking problems and air it was becoming a chore to breathe. There was a lot of handwringing over the problem, but nobody did much about it, least of all Congress, which was reluctant to spend the money. They were finally goaded into action on November 11, 1921.

Congress had planned to honor the men who died in the late Great War by bringing back the body of a fallen unidentified soldier from a battlefield in France. He would become, in a tomb at the entrance to Arlington National Cemetery, just across the Potomac River in Virginia, the symbol of all the men who gave their lives for their country. The ceremony began a few days before Armistice Day,1921, when the body lay in state in the Rotunda of the Capitol. After a morning of speechmaking, all the assembled dignitaries, many of them representatives of America's allies in the war, took part in a motorcade that was planned through Potomac Park and across the only bridge spanning the river, a highway bridge that led to the general vicinity of the cemetery. But before they ever reached the bridge they got caught in a traffic jam. The Unknown Soldier made it across, though it took more than two hours, but many of the officials, citing previous engagements, dropped out along the way.

The following May, the Lincoln Memorial was finally dedicated, and once again there were traffic jams of monumental proportions. And Congressmen who participated in the ceremonies made it a point to keep their backs to the riverbank, which hadn't been improved due to lack of funds. Two weeks later, they voted the funds and two years later, in 1924, approved plans for a stone bridge across the Potomac from the Lincoln Memorial to Arlington. At the same time, they approved yet another committee to make suggestions on making Washington a more beautiful, and more functional, city. It was welcome news to most Washingtonians because the "city beautiful" movement had never dealt with the problems that would come when the urban landscape was littered with cars, trucks and excursion buses.

The committee didn't have an easy time of it. They couldn't stop the widening of streets and avenues and the removal of street trees to make it possible. They didn't have the funds to expand parks, though they had plenty of plans for them. But they did have power, if not money, and influential men all over the country made pilgrimages to the capital to give them moral support. In the process, making the national capital a beautiful place to live became, by 1930, a national priority as Americans finally stopped complaining about spending federal funds for the benefit of the residents of a single city. For the first time in its history, Washington D.C., in 1930, became the property of, and a source of pride to, all the people.

Washingtonians, both the temporary and permanent kind, had been insulated from many of the problems other Americans faced. They had experienced racial problems for generations, but the ups and downs of the economy that affected every other city never touched Washington as seriously. But when America welcomed Washington into the community of cities in 1930, Washington also got a taste of some of the problems that had been affecting its sister cities all along. In 1931, as the Great Depression was settling in, Congress approved a big public works program for the District and, in addition to getting needed improvement, Washington became the only city in the United States where unemployment actually dropped after the collapse of the stock market. Life in the capital was on such an upbeat note that the National Symphony Orchestra announced its inaugural season and sold every subscription. The local Board of Trade announced a record year and the Visitors' Association logged more conventions than any year since it began promoting tourism.

Then in the spring the door to the rest of the country was flung open and a chilling blast came in. It had happened before, most notably in 1894, when a contingent of unemployed men marched on Washington looking for jobs. The papers called them "Coxey's Army" because they were led by Jacob Coxey of Ohio. They didn't get what they came for, but they did cause a riot outside the Capitol. It ended when General Coxey was arrested for walking on the grass and his followers were dispersed by mounted police. Many of them stayed in Washington afterward and were finally given train tickets home by an embarrassed government. The army that Washington officials saw coming in May, 1932 was similar, but different. It was composed of veterans of World War I, who announced that they were on their way to petition Congress for a bonus that had been promised to them but wasn't due for payment for another 15 years. Most of these men had been thrown out of work by the Depression and needed the money right away. Their march,

which had begun on the West Coast, was well publicized, and everywhere along the way they picked up new recruits. By the time they arrived there were 20,000 of them. The head of the Metropolitan Police was ready for them. He had arranged in advance for them to be billeted in empty buildings around town, and had arranged with the Army to loan him tents to take care of the overload. He had ordered his men not to harass them and had enlisted the help of local citizens to make them as comfortable as was possible. All the marchers had been in the military, so it was easy for them to adapt to military-style discipline. There was no riot, nor even the hint of one, and the people of the city were able, for the first time, to get a close look at their fellow Americans and get a better idea of what was going on out there.

The so-called Bonus Army camped in Washington for about a month. Not long after they arived, the House of Representatives voted to pay them the money they had coming to them. President Hoover announced that if the Senate did the same thing, he'd veto the legislation. He didn't have to. The Senate killed the measure before he had the chance. As it had done with Coxey's Army, the government offered to buy train tickets for the marchers who didn't have any other way to get home, but many refused the offer, pointing out that they didn't have any home to go to. Once they decided to stay, their families joined them. And other bonus-seekers, convinced that Congress would see the error of its ways, joined them, too.

Just before the session ended, several hundred of them picketed the Capitol non-stop for sixty hours. To make sure that none of them would sleep on the grass there, officials ordered the sprinklers turned on and left on. Congress responded at last by voting $300 million for unemployment relief, but stipulated that the money should be divided by individual states. The picketers knew they'd probably starve before they ever saw any of the money, and so they decided to stick it out in Washington. There was no money to feed them, no jobs to give them. The President said it was the District's problem, District officials felt otherwise. But it was clear that somebody was going to have to do something. The police were ordered to get rid of them by August 1. Fortunately, a nearby estate was donated as the site of a new encampment, and before the deadline all but a few hundred of the 10,000 campers had been removed. Then trouble began. As the police were ushering a contingent from a building, one of the Bonus Marchers tossed a brick at them. A minor riot followed, but was ended quickly when one of the march leaders shouted that it was lunch time. That gave the police time to regroup, and for word to get around that there was trouble brewing. By mid-afternoon, the president felt compelled to restore order by calling out the troops.

Two hours later a cavalry unit, with sabers drawn, began marching down Constitution Avenue behind their leader, General Douglas MacArthur. Behind them was a contingent of infantry, followed by a fleet of six tanks commanded by Major Dwight D. Eisenhower. When they reached the Bonus Army's camp, they fired tear gas at the protesters, and when they had them on the run moved on to the next camp to play out their drama all over again. When they reached the main camp on the Anacostia River, the tanks took possession of the bridge while the troops burned the camp to the ground.

There was no television in those days and only Washingtonians could see what had happened, but the events of that summer day caused a stir in the country that took everyone's mind away from the Depression for a few weeks. The Hoover administration defended itself by saying that, while the bulk of the Bonus Marchers were veterans of the war, they were led by Communists, who were the ones responsible for all that trouble. General MacArthur felt compelled to state that his actions, though harsh, were inspired by no less a fact than that the government itself was in grave peril. Washingtonians, who traditionally kept their nose out of what official Washington was up to, themselves began to protest.

It all became a moot point because, a few days before the Bonus Army was run out of town, the Depression was ushered in with a cut in the salaries of government workers and unpaid furloughs for many. The District's operating budget was cut proportionately, which dried up other jobs. By the beginning of 1933, when Franklin Roosevelt took his oath of office on the Capitol's East Portico, it was estimated that 200,000 people who lived nearby were without a way to make a living.

Within days the mood changed. The Roosevelts, it seemed, were going to make nice neighbors. Within ten days of his new administration, the president had managed to get the country's banks,

including 20 in the District of Columbia, back on their feet again. Government salaries were reduced again, but there was a new energy in town and people were once more smiling and hopeful. And they were getting new neighbors, lots of them. Washington was the headquarters of the New Deal and the president was bringing in what he considered the best minds in the country to bring on the new world. At first, the New Dealers and the old Washington observed each other at arm's length, and each decided that the other was a necessary evil, but little more. For their part, the natives felt put upon. A government ruling that made it illegal for husbands and wives to work for federal agencies at the same time put a lot of them out of work. And though the number of jobs expanded by more than a third, they were filled mostly by people new to Washington. But there was a bright side. Unlike other cities, Washington was rebounding from the Depression at an astonishing rate. It was virtually impossible to get a hotel room, and houses that had been standing empty were easy to rent again. And there were new people arriving every day with money to spend. The local economy was the best in the country in 1936, in spite of federal pay cuts, and the average income of a Washingtonian was nearly double that of a New Yorker. Neither Washingtonians nor New Yorkers were getting rich, but they were surviving at last.

The work of improving and expanding the city began again soon afterward. During the decade of the '30s some 800 new office buildings and nearly 2,500 new houses were built. Among the structures added was the long-planned National Gallery of Art and a new wing for the Library of Congress. More trees were planted and lawns established, and it seemed entire quarries of marble were being exhausted to keep up with progress in the District of Columbia. Washingtonians had new sources of pride everywhere they turned. But there were still little problems to be overcome. The time had come, it seemed, to add a memorial to Thomas Jefferson. The architect John Russell Pope submitted plans for a structure on the Tidal Basin that would be an adaptation of Jefferson's own design for the Rotunda at the University of Virginia, itself an adaptation of the Pantheon in Rome. In spite of its antecendents, experts across the country said it was the silliest thing they had ever seen. Nothing was right about it in their eyes. It would interrupt the view of the Potomac from the White House, said some. Its dome was completely out of place, said others.

Environmentalists complained that if it were ever built, the Japanese cherry trees would be destroyed. The controversy raged for more than five years before construction actually began in 1939, and when workmen arrived to begin the job they found people had chained themselves to the cherry trees in a last-ditch effort to stop them. The problems were eventually worked out and the memorial to Mr. Jefferson, surrounded by cherry trees, fits into the cityscape so perfectly that visitors can't help wondering what all the fuss was about.

During the boom of the 1930s, people who lived in the District of Columbia joined their fellow Americans in a new phenomonen. They began to move to the suburbs. Among the new agencies of the New Deal, the Federal Housing Administration made it easier for wage earners to get mortgages for homes. Better roads had already been built, and by 1936 middle-class Washingtonians were moving in huge numbers to new housing developments across the river in Virginia. Those who didn't need low-cost mortgages moved into the plusher surroundings of Chevy Chase in Maryland.

Soon the government itself began to follow them, first into Bethesda, Maryland, and then into other nearby communities, making it possible for people there to get good jobs without commuting. It was an idea that would become commonplace in urban centers twenty or thirty years later.

Another idea pioneered in the District at the same time was urban renewal. The Colonial village of Georgetown, which was already established when the Federal City moved in, had become a slum over the years, and though most of its old houses were still standing, nobody considered them to be worth much. But if it was run down, it still had plenty of charm, and even before the New Deal arrived in town people were buying Georgetown houses and restoring them. Mrs. Roosevelt took an interest in the area, and people her husband was attracting to Washington took her advice. By the end of the decade, the neighborhood was completely "gentrified," and real estate values were doubled, tripled and more.

There was a certain charm to all of Washington in the 1930s. Threats of war in Europe prompted many intellectuals to migrate to the United States and they found the climate that suited them best in the capital. Scientific research had been a government priority since Jefferson's day, but in the post-Depression years private research groups based themselves in the Washington area, and the educational community was growing both in size and stature. The city had always had the heady mix of foreign influence, thanks to the diplomatic community, but now there was a new ingredient, and the cosmopolitan atmosphere in the District of Columbia would have amazed the men who served there a century before and couldn't wait to go home.

Washington was home to some of the best minds in the country and, even though governments would come and go, most of them were there to stay. World events were conspiring to give them plenty of stimulating company in the years ahead. As the Nazi juggernaut began marching across Europe in 1939 and 1940, official Washington knew that it signalled the end of the New Deal and the beginning of something brand-new.

People who had been making their living keeping track of such projects as the Works Progress Administration found new jobs in things like Lend-Lease, aimed at helping European countries defend themselves. And, as had happened back in 1917, the District once again welcomed "dollar-a-year men," business leaders serving the government for the most minimum of minimum wages. During the years of the New Deal such people had stayed away from Washington, which they considered a hotbed of Socialistic ideas that were bad for business. War, on the other hand, even somebody else's war, is good for business. And even though they more often than not joined the cause for isolation, they were busily converting their factories from the production of consumer goods, and Congress was busily appropriating money to buy the guns and airplanes they were beginning to produce. In the process, unemployment virtually disappeared around the country, and the power that made the wheels turn centered on the District of Columbia.

As the defense effort was gathering steam, the city administrators were still trying to obtain funds to get rid of the temporary structures that had lined the Mall since the last World War, more than 20 years before. Instead, Congress gave them money to build more of them. To handle the increased traffic, both from the influx of new people and the opening of National Airport in 1941, streets were widened again, some parkland was eliminated, and people who had seen such progress before began to wonder if Washington would ever become a city beautiful.

Meanwhile, the War Department was growing

faster than any agency in town. It was clear that a building was needed to house all those generals and admirals. It was clear that there was no room in the District of Columbia for such a massive building. The site they selected was in Arlington, at the end of the new bridge between the Lincoln Memorial and the Tomb of the Unknown Soldier. No one remembered, apparently, the recent battle over the possibility that the Jefferson Memorial would spoil the vista from the White House to the river. But the District Planning Commission stepped in and convinced the Secretary of War that his new pentagon-shaped building would be just as functional if it were located further down the river, even though the president and members of Congress might not see it every time they looked out the window. Possibly a strong argument in that direction came from the fact that much of the day-to-day work of the War Department was being handled from a double row of wooden buildings on both sides of the reflecting pool in the center of the Mall.

During the years just before the United States officially got into the war, Washington became an exciting place to be. There were more young people there than ever before, and all of them had a strong sense of purpose. If they worked hard, they played just as hard, and the 1939 and 1940 social seasons were as exciting as any the District had ever seen. During the day official Washington was dealing with massive problems, but in the evening the only problem they faced was "the servant problem." There were so many good jobs available, nobody was signing on as domestic help any longer, and the new Washingtonians were sometimes forced to refresh their own drinks at cocktail parties.

Then, at the end of 1941, the mood changed. On December 8, the United States declared war on Japan, and three days later Germany and Italy declared war on the United States. The "defense" program became known as the "war" program, and the capital lost much of its gaiety. Even though the mobilization for war has since been hailed as astonishing, the toll on the people of Washington has often been overlooked. Everyone in the city lived from day to day knowing that what they did was crucial to the future of the world. The city, already bursting at the seams, was being overwhelmed by new arrivals. Shortages of gasoline made locating out of town impractical, but locating housing within the District was nearly impossible. They faced the fact that they were living in a prime target for air raids and suffered through nightly blackouts. It

didn't matter all that much. The average government employee worked a minimum of ten hours a day, many even longer. Compared to life in other world capitals at the time, theirs was a life of beer and skittles. Yet no other American city was as closely touched, or its mood as affected, by World War II as Washington, D.C.

The mood was somber in Washington through the middle of 1944, when the fortunes of war finally seemed to tilt toward the Allied cause. Even then life was far from pleasant, and everyone knew it would be that way until it was "over over there." When it finally was over, in August, 1945, the lights went back on again, rationing ended, and as Washington's sons began appearing around town in civilian clothes, the city was ready to get down to the job of getting things back to normal.

The years following World War II were kinder to the District of Columbia than the years following other wars, but getting back to normal wasn't easy for Washingtonians. The problems facing the city's black population couldn't be swept under the rug any longer; there were slums to be cleared, parks to be rebuilt, highways to be added. And, as happened to other cities in postwar America, the population was shifting out of town. In the 1950s, the District's population fell by more than 36 percent. Yet, though some of the problems Washingtonians faced 30 years ago are still plaguing them, the quality of life in the capital was better than ever, and when the Kennedy administration hit town in 1961 to establish his "New Frontier," Washington was never less a frontier town.

Among the legacies of the war were longer sessions for Congress, which meant that Senators and Representatives didn't find boardinghouse living as convenient. In earlier days, they had been able to spend a few months in Washington and the rest of the year back home with their constituents and their families. Many of them tried to maintain two separate homes, but it became increasingly difficult, and by the 1950s it was a foregone conclusion that, if you were going to serve in Congress, you'd better plan to move your family to Washington. Since Congress functioned as a city council for the District, it was good news for the neighborhood.

Washington had always buzzed when there was a crisis, but when Congress wasn't in session, or sometimes even when it was, the only buzzing came from clouds of mosquitoes. But somewhere between the war and the arrival of the New Frontier, the buzzing became continuous. It was the sound of power.

In quieter times, power was just as important to politicians as it is today. But the world has changed and the Washington merry-go-round is spinning faster than ever. There is always somebody who thinks he can do the job better and is just waiting for a chance. There is a press corps on the job around the clock every day of the year, there are constituents who don't think twice about picking up the phone, or even catching the next flight for an eyeball-to-eyeball encounter. Washington is a place where "contacts" count for everything, but friendships are rare. It's where nobody does anybody any favors if they think they won't be remembered. And repaid.

Yet, just as planning next year's state fair begins the day after this year's ends, a president no sooner takes his oath of office than dozens in the audience begin weighing plans to take his place. Members of Congress spend as much time working on keeping their seats as filling them. And all the bureaucrats work just as hard to keep their jobs, in spite of the pressure, the frustration, the uncertainty. Living in Washington has that effect. In fact, when a long-time public servant is beaten at the polls, it's a fair bet that the capital won't lose a citizen but gain a new lobbyist or powerful lawyer.

Over the last several decades, the tone of the city seems to have been set by the occupant of the White House, and whether the tone is good or bad is largely in the eye of the beholder. But the president's circle, though large, isn't the only one that influences life in the District of Columbia. The press corps is larger and includes representatives from as many foreign countries as the diplomatic corps. There are more than 350,000 people in Washington who don't mind being called bureaucrats. The intelligence community, by its nature, is uncounted, but certainly needs to be taken into account in assessing who's important. And who could be more important

than the military? They are there by the thousands. And there are the ordinary Washingtonians, the people who work in what officials call "the private sector" to make sure that visitors are made comfortable, the Metro system runs on time, and that those people coming to town to chat with their personal representative in Congress get to the right place at the right time.

It's a city like any other. It has the same problems with its schools and its water supply that other American cities experience. Neighbors have disagreements with each other. The local football team loses games once in a while. It gets steamy in the summer and clammy cold in the winter. But, for all its similarities, Washington, D.C. is as unique among American cities as it is among the capitals of the world. If its function didn't set it apart, its name would. It was designated a district by the men who conceived it as a place apart, separated from any of the states. It belongs to all the people of every state.

Many of the celebrations that lift the spirits of Washingtonians each year are national celebrations, like the presidential inaugural held every four years. Every year they turn out to mark Robert E. Lee's birthday in January and Abraham Lincoln's birthday less than a month later. They celebrate George Washington's birthday with a Revolutionary War encampment and Saint Patrick's Day with a parade down Constitution Avenue. The Easter Egg Roll is held on the White House lawn a week or two after the cherry blossoms bloom. They have special programs for William Shakespeare's birthday in April, and in the summer the Marine Band and the Army Band give free outdoor concerts every week. On Sunday afternoons Washingtonians can watch polo games on the Mall. And on July Fourth ... well, where else can you expect a more colorful celebration? It's like that all year long. Washington thrives on ceremony and celebrations. And, as it nears its 200th anniversary, the future is looking terrific. Why else would so many people go to so much trouble to keep on living there?

Facing page: the Washington Monument.

IN THIS TEMPLE
AS IN THE HEARTS OF THE PEOPLE
FOR WHOM HE SAVED THE UNION
THE MEMORY OF ABRAHAM LINCOLN
IS ENSHRINED FOREVER

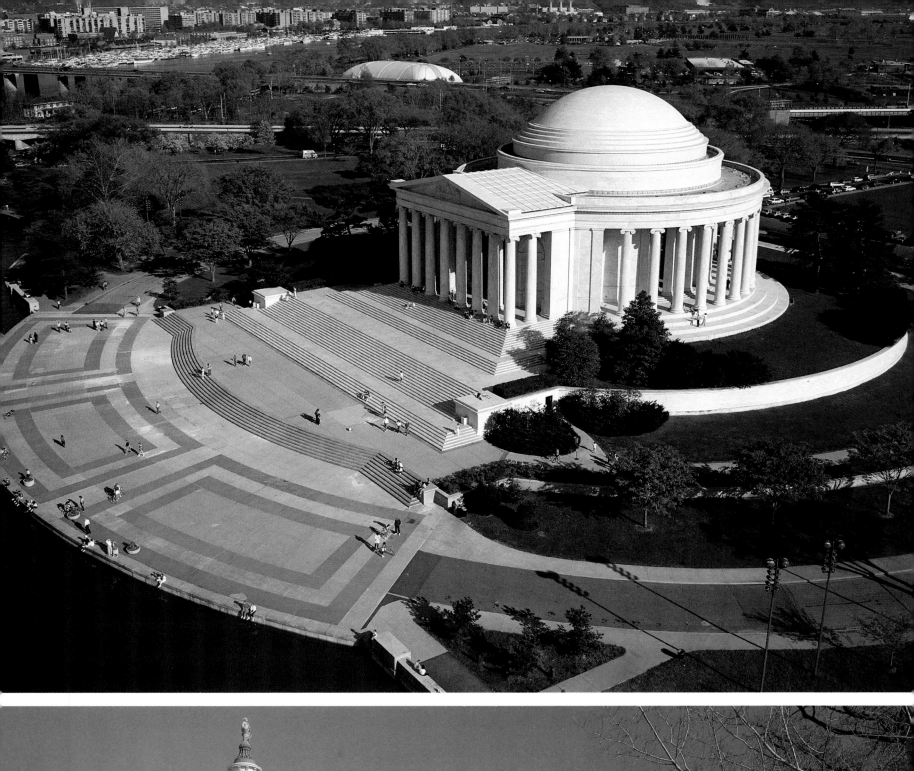

George Washington officiated at the ceremony when the cornerstone of the United States Capitol (previous pages left top, facing page bottom and above) was laid in 1793. Designed in 1792 by Dr. William Thornton to exhibit, according to Washington, "Grandeur, Simplicity and Convenience," the Capitol is crowned by a tiered dome and topped by Thomas Crawford's bronze Statue of Freedom. Previous pages left bottom and facing page top: the low dome and classical portico of the Jefferson Memorial and (previous pages right) the imposing statue and inscription in the Lincoln Memorial. Top: the statue of Benito Juarez outside the Watergate Complex, and (right) the Washington Monument.

The 19-foot-high portrait statue of Thomas Jefferson (right) in the Jefferson Memorial is set on a floor of pink and gray Tennessee marble within walls of white Georgia marble. Sculpted by Rudolph Evans, the statue was represented by a plaster model at the dedication ceremony in 1943, and could not be cast in bronze for several years because of wartime restrictions on the use of metal. The 21 floors of the 1935 National Archives (below) provide safe housing for thousands of priceless historical documents and records, including the Declaration of Independence and its Bill of Rights, and the US Constitution. Facing page: lancet arches and ribbed vaulting in the nave of Washington National Cathedral. Begun in 1907, this is built of limestone in the Gothic style of the 14th century. Overleaf: the Hirshhorn Sculpture Garden.

Facing page: (top left) figures in the Hirshhorn Sculpture Garden, and (top right) lunch break in a city park. (Bottom right) part of the extensive and colorful collection of Victoriana in the Arts and Industries Building. A number of the items on display – from horse-drawn carriages and furniture to ornate pistols and French lace – were exhibited in the Philadelphia Exposition of 1876. The building, designed by Cluss and Schule in 1880 and restored in 1976, is itself an elaborate Queen Anne Victorian creation. (Bottom left) a Foucault Pendulum, which demonstrates the earth's rotation by knocking down red pegs, in the National Museum of American History, and (above) the vast, free-standing globe in the National Geographic Explorers Hall, on the ground floor of the National Geographic Society headquarters. Left: patient metro commuters.

Three Vietnam serviceman (above), depicted in bronze by sculptor Frederick Hart, provide a striking complement to the long, simple line of the Vietnam Veterans Memorial (facing page), dedicated in 1982. A national competition held to find a suitable monument to the Southeast Asian War's American dead attracted over a thousand submissions, from which the jury chose that of Maya Ying Lin, a 21-year-old Yale architecture senior. She describes the memorial as "... a rift in the earth – a long polished black stone wall, emerging and receding into the earth," on which are inscribed 58,007 names in chronological order of death.

Two of Washington's most imposing yet serene monuments face each other across the Tidal Basin. The Washington Monument (facing page) came into being gradually between 1848 and 1885, following the success of Robert Mills' entry in a national competition held by the 1836 Monument Committee to provide the capital with a suitable memorial to its founder. Mills' original plans called for an elaborately-decorated marble obelisk, to be fronted by a circular, Greek-style temple and a great marble statue of Washington driving a *quadriga.*. The simple, white tower of today is, fortunately, all that the committee's funds and public opinion would run to. Above: the cool, Ionic columns of the Jefferson Memorial, designed by John Russell Pope and completed in 1942.

Top: flowers and fountains and (above) athletes and balloons in the Market Square of the 18th-century port of Alexandria, Virginia, just south of Washington, D.C. The fine Gothic-Revival Smithsonian Institution Building (facing page top), built of red Seneca sandstone and housing the Institute's administrative offices, is familiarly known as "the Castle." Facing page bottom: the stately Jefferson Memorial, whose shallow dome and circular shape once earned it the irreverent title of "Jefferson's muffin."

The Old Patent Office building, built between 1836 and 1867 under the supervision of Robert Mills, also housed displays of patent models and artworks, and in the Great Hall (facing page), President and Mrs. Lincoln received their guests at the second inaugural ball. In 1962, having recently been saved from demolition, the Office became the home of two Smithsonian museums, the National Museum of American Art and the National Portrait Gallery. A replica of the Parthenon in Virginia freestone, this Greek-Revival building and its pillared marble galleries provide a stately setting for the museum exhibits. Among these is Gilbert Stuart's painting of George Washington (right), National Portrait Gallery. Above: the tomb and memorial of James Smithson, founder of the Smithsonian Institution, in the Crypt Room of the Smithsonian Institution Building.

Right: José Riviera's "Infinity" outside the National Museum of History and Technology. The National Air and Space Museum (remaining pictures) contains exhibits spanning the whole history of man's longing for and attainment of flight. Above: the Apollo Lunar Landing Module and (top right) the docking Apollo and Soyuz rockets.

The "Apotheosis of Washington," which crowns the dome (above) of the United States Capitol, was painted by Constantino Brumidi, who, by then almost 60, worked on his masterpiece for 11 months and signed it in 1865. He painted in fresco, by which pigment is applied to freshly-troweled plaster, each section having to be completed before the plaster dries. The encircling frieze, on which Brumidi was engaged at his death in 1880, depicts dramatic events in American history. Facing page: the Capitol's Statuary Hall, restored to appear as it did when the House met there between 1807 and 1857. Since 1864, it has been a showcase for statues of America's great men and women, each state allowed by law to supply two such distinguished sculptures. Overleaf: the Jefferson Memorial reflected in the Tidal Basin.

The George Washington Masonic National Memorial (facing page and bottom right), standing at the west end of King Street in Alexandria, is a shrine greatly revered by Freemasons from all over the world. Facing page: (top) the Memorial Museum, containing much Washington memorabilia, and (bottom) the bronze statue of George Washington by Bryant Baker, portraying him as Worshipful Master of his lodge, set between the polished green granite pillars of the Memorial Hall. Behind these, one of Allyn Cox's murals depicts General Washington attending a service in Christ Church, Philadelphia, in 1778. Right and bottom: elegant townhouses, and (below) Wisconsin Avenue, in Georgetown.

The Old Pension Building was designed in 1883 by
General Montgomery Meigs after the Palazzo Farnese
in Italy. From its enclosed central courtyard (top),
roofed in sky blue to suggest its open Italian
prototype, radiate offices where, for some 40 years,
clerks administered the pensions of war veterans.
These now house the National Building Museum.
Above and right: the ornate Library of Congress
Building, and (facing page) the National Gallery of Art.

Washington's buildings have been designed on a grand scale and after classic architectural principles in keeping with its role as the nation's capital. The Supreme Court Building (above), completed in 1935, was designed by Cass Gilbert to be "a building of dignity and importance suitable for its use as the permanent home of the Supreme Court of the United States" and built in the style of classical Greece, its great portico supported by massive Corinthian order columns. Facing page top: the fine Gothic Smithsonian Institution Building, built in 1849 as the Institution's first building, and (right) Daniel Burnham's Beaux-Arts Union Station, a monument to the railroads and now the National Visitor Center. Arlington Memorial Amphitheater (facing page bottom), finished in white Vermont marble, honors the American Army, Navy and Marine Corps. In front of it stands the Tomb of the Unknowns (overleaf left). Overleaf right: simple headstones in the 1,100 acres of Arlington Cemetery.

Previous pages: (left) the National Air and Space Museum and (right) the National Archives. Above: the National Statuary Hall, and (top) Daniel Chester French's statue of Abraham Lincoln, Lincoln Memorial. Top right: General Andrew Jackson in Lafayette Square and (right) the White House.

The Executive Office Building (right), built in the extravagantly-ornate style of the French Second Empire as the State, War and Navy Building, was the world's biggest office building on its completion in 1888. Two miles of corridor connect 550 rooms, and the exterior is adorned with 900 doric columns. This extraordinary building now houses the Office of Management and Budget and most of the President's White House staff. The National Museum of Natural History (below), part of the Smithsonian Institution, presents an incredible range of exhibits from the natural world. Facing page: (bottom) sightseers on the Mall, and (top) the bright mosaic Byzantine dome and the Knights' Tower of the National Shrine of the Immaculate Conception. Overleaf: the Main Reading Room in the Jefferson Building of the Library of Congress.

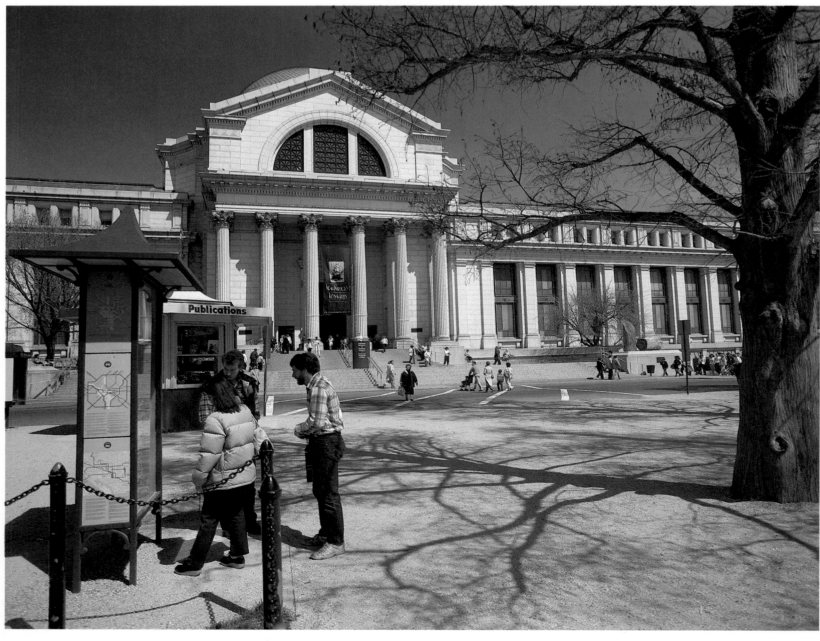

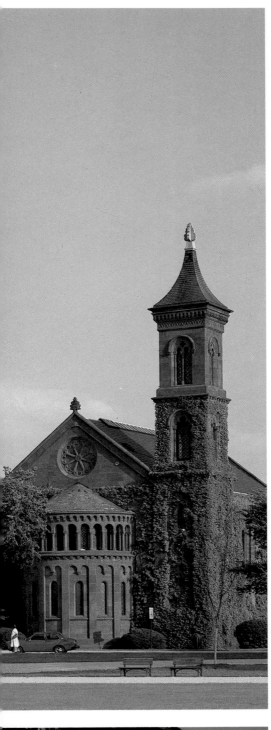

Top left: the Smithsonian Institution Building, (far left) old Union Station, (left) the National Museum of Natural History, and (above and top) the East Building of the National Gallery of Art.

The National Museum of Natural History (these pages) contains millions of exhibits – live and mounted specimens, models, dioramas, recreations and artifacts – designed for the study of the natural world. Top: the largest recorded African bush elephant.

A city of memorials, Washington, D.C. honors America's great and her brave. Top left: the Jefferson Memorial, (center left) the Washington Monument, (above center) the Spencer Fullerton Baird statue, (above) the J. F. Kennedy grave, (facing page bottom left) Arlington National Cemetery, and (facing page bottom right) crowds outside Arlington Memorial Amphitheater. Top: the Petersen House, where Abraham Lincoln died. Left and facing page top: the United States Capitol.

"Erected of enduring materials, our temple will stand throughout the ages. It will carry to generations yet unborn, and to those to whom we may seem an ancient race, the message of human brotherhood. It will perpetuate the attributes of self-denial, patriotism, love of country and fellow man, which were typified in the life and work of the great Mason, the master-builder of our nation – George Washington." This is the spirit in which the George Washington Masonic National Memorial (these pages) was erected and is maintained, honoring the first president and presenting a fascinating display of his possessions in the Memorial Museum (above).

Ground was broken for the Chesapeake and Ohio Canal (this page and facing page top) in 1828, and for the rest of the century it carried goods between Columbus and Georgetown (these pages). Facing page bottom: the atrium of Georgetown Park.

Overleaf: three of the capital's most familiar landmarks - (left) the United States Capitol, (right top) the White House and (right bottom) the Washington Monument.

Above: Ford's Theater, scene of the assassination of Abraham Lincoln on 14 April, 1865. Shot by the actor John Wilkes Booth, Lincoln died the following morning. The theater, closed for over 100 years, is again in use. Exhibits in the city's art galleries (remaining pictures) include the bronze Mercury (left) attributed to Adriaen de Vries, cast c.1603-1613, and (far right) "Watson and the Shark" (1778) by John Singleton Copley, both in the National Gallery of Art. Right: a carving in the Children's Chapel of Washington National Cathedral.

Previous pages: tulips and wisteria outside the National Museum of American History. These pages: parades on Constitution Avenue during the Cherry Blossom Festival, which takes place annually in the first week of April in celebration of the flowering of thousands of Japanese cherry trees planted around the Tidal Basin in West Potomac Park, along the roadside in East Potomac Park and in the grounds of the Washington Monument. These trees were given as a gift of friendship from the city of Tokyo to the city of Washington in 1912 and include specimens of 12 varieties. Those planted around the Tidal Basin are mostly Yoshina, which bears a profusion of white, single blooms, together with some Akebono, whose single blossoms are pale pink. Many of the East Potomac Park trees are Kwanzan and bear heavy clusters of double, deep-pink blooms.

Facing page: the pale, sharp lines of the Washington Mormon Temple in Kensington, Maryland, and (above) intricate decoration and warm gold in the National Shrine of the Immaculate Conception in Washington, D.C. Built between 1914 and 1959 with money raised in parishes all over America, this Marian shrine, "speaks ... with the voice of all the sons and daughters of America, who came here from the various countries of the old world, who came together around the heart of a mother they all had in common" (Pope John Paul II). Both Byzantine and Romanesque elements are incorporated into its great cruciform structure, and the lavish interior includes John DeRosen's "Christ in Majesty" mosaic in the North Apse of the Upper Church (above).

This page: exhibits in the Hirshhorn Museum and Sculpture Garden, built in 1974 to house the collection of self-made millionaire Joseph Hirshhorn. Below: Alexander Calder's "Two Discs", (below left) "Torso Fruit" and "The Therapeutist" by Jean Arp, and the painting "Delusions of Grandeur" by the Surrealist René Magritte and (above left) "Painted Steel Rainfall." Facing page top: the bronze Mercury (left) attributed to Adriaen de Vries in the rotunda of the National Gallery of Art. Facing page bottom: a Baldwin locomotive, on show as part of the display of American Victoriana which recreates the spirit of the 1876 Philadelphia Exposition in the Arts and Industries Building.

Rows of spring flowers color the settings of Washington's celebrated white buildings. Facing page: the Gothic pinnacles and flying buttresses of Washington National Cathedral, (top left) the Netherlands Carillon, on the Marine Memorial grounds of Arlington National Cemetery, (top) the Washington Monument, (left) the Watergate Complex and (above) Union Station, now the National Visitor Center. Overleaf: (left) a memorial to the crew of the Space Shuttle *Challenger* and (right) the missile pit in the Space Hall, both in the National Air and Space Museum.

IN MEMORIAM

CREW OF SPACE SHUTTLE MISSION 51-L *CHALLENGER*, JANUARY 28, 1986

The crew of *Challenger* was lost as a result of an in-flight explosion, shortly after the launch of the Space Shuttle.

(back row, left to right)

Ellison S. Onizuka, mission specialist. Born June 24, 1946, Keilakekua, Kona, Hawaii. He became a NASA astronaut in 1978.

S. Christa Corrigan McAuliffe, teacher. Born September 2, 1948, Boston, Massachusetts. She was selected as the primary candidate for the Teacher in Space project in July 1985.

Gregory B. Jarvis, payload specialist. Born August 24, 1944, Detroit, Michigan. He was selected as a payload specialist from Hughes Aircraft Corp. in 1984.

Judith A. Resnik, mission specialist. Born April 15, 1949, Akron, Ohio. She became a NASA astronaut in 1978.

(front row, left to right)

Michael J. Smith, pilot. Born April 30, 1945, Beaufort, North Carolina. He became a NASA astronaut in 1980.

Francis R. (Dick) Scobee, spacecraft commander. Born May 19, 1939, Cle Elum, Washington. He became a NASA astronaut in 1978.

Ronald E. McNair, mission specialist. Born October 21, 1950, Lake City, South Carolina. He became a NASA astronaut in 1978.

WE HOLD THESE TRUTHS TO BE SELF-
EVIDENT: THAT ALL MEN ARE CREATED
EQUAL, THAT THEY ARE ENDOWED BY THEIR
CREATOR WITH CERTAIN INALIENABLE
RIGHTS, AMONG THESE ARE LIFE, LIBERTY
AND THE PURSUIT OF HAPPINESS, THAT
TO SECURE THESE RIGHTS GOVERNMENTS
ARE INSTITUTED AMONG MEN. WE···
SOLEMNLY PUBLISH AND DECLARE, THAT
THESE COLONIES ARE AND OF RIGHT
OUGHT TO BE FREE AND INDEPENDENT
STATES····AND FOR THE SUPPORT OF THIS
DECLARATION, WITH A FIRM RELIANCE
ON THE PROTECTION OF DIVINE
PROVIDENCE, WE MUTUALLY PLEDGE
OUR LIVES, OUR FORTUNES AND OUR
SACRED HONOUR.

The United States Capitol (top and left) stands at the head of the Mall, facing the Washington Monument (overleaf: left and right top). On either side of this are set the Jefferson Memorial (top left and far right) and the White House (overleaf right bottom). Above: Explorers Hall, National Geographic Society headquarters. Right: the Iwo Jima Memorial.

LET EVERY NATION KNOW
WHETHER IT WISHES US WELL OR ILL
THAT WE SHALL PAY ANY PRICE · BEAR ANY BURD
MEET ANY HARDSHIP · SUPPORT ANY FRIEN
OPPOSE ANY FOE TO ASSURE THE SURVIV
AND THE SUCCESS OF LIBERTY

THE ENERGY · THE FAITH · THE DEVOTION
WHICH WE BRING TO THIS ENDEAVOR
WILL LIGHT OUR COUNTRY
AND ALL WHO SERVE IT
AND THE GLOW FROM THAT FIRE
CAN TRULY LIGHT THE WORLD

PLEASE
KEEP OFF
WALL

Previous pages: a café and specialty shops in the Pavilion at the Old Post Office. Facing page: words from President John F. Kennedy's inaugural address, engraved on a low wall at his grave site in Arlington National Cemetery. This page: guarding the Tomb of the Unknowns, Arlington National Cemetery.

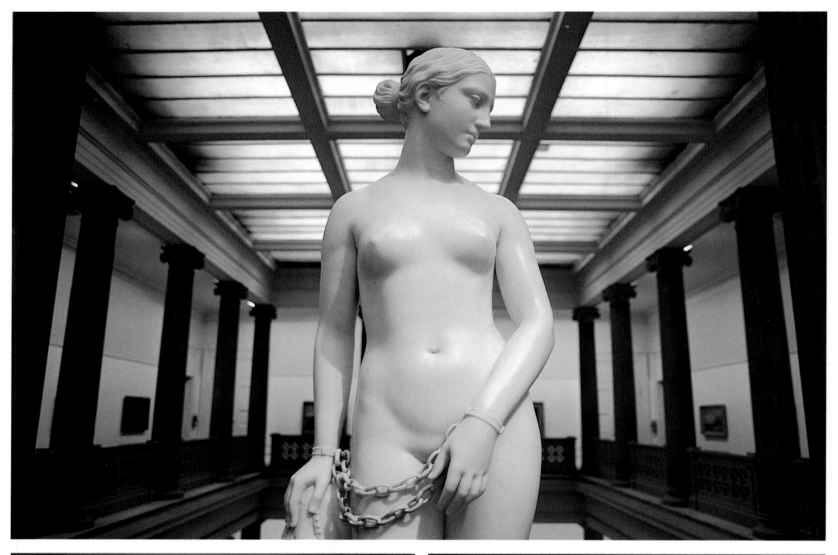

Top: Hiram Powers' "The Greek Slave" (1843) in the Corcoran Gallery, based on the collection of William Wilson Corcoran. Above: the Octagon Room and (left) the Grand Salon in the Renwick Gallery, part of the Smithsonian National Museum of American Art. Facing page: the National Museum of American Art.

Top: the White House, (top right) the Lincoln Memorial, (right) the Washington Monument and (far right) the United States Capitol, floodlit. Above center: Stars and Stripes at the base of the Washington Monument and (above) Dulles International Airport, at evening.

The collection now housed in the Smithsonian National Museum of American History (these pages) began in 1858 when the US Patent Office removed its accumulation of curiosities to the Smithsonian. Now, this museum offers a fascinating record of America's past. The first floor highlights her scientific and technological achievements, including those in transportation such as a Conestoga 1840s covered wagon (above), the 1851 *Pioneer* passenger locomotive (below), and the steam passenger locomotive No. 1401(facing page top), built in 1926, a 1913 Harley Davidson motorcycle (left) and an antique automobile (facing page bottom). The second floor concentrates on social and political history, while the third floor features a miscellany of exhibits including displays of coins, stamps, glass, ceramics and studies of communications and photography. Above left: a reconstruction of an early newspaper bureau, and (below left) a depiction of Roger Fenton, the first professional photo journalist, photographing wartime subjects at the time of the Crimean War (1853-1856), both on the third floor.

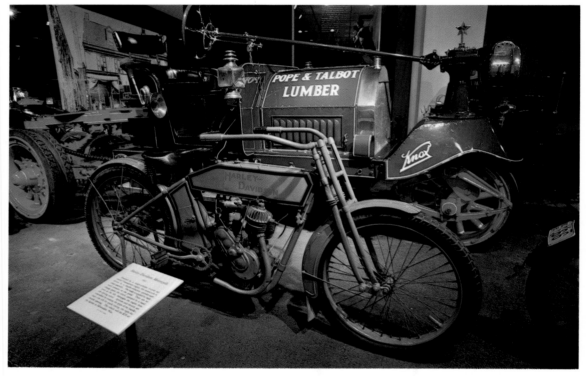

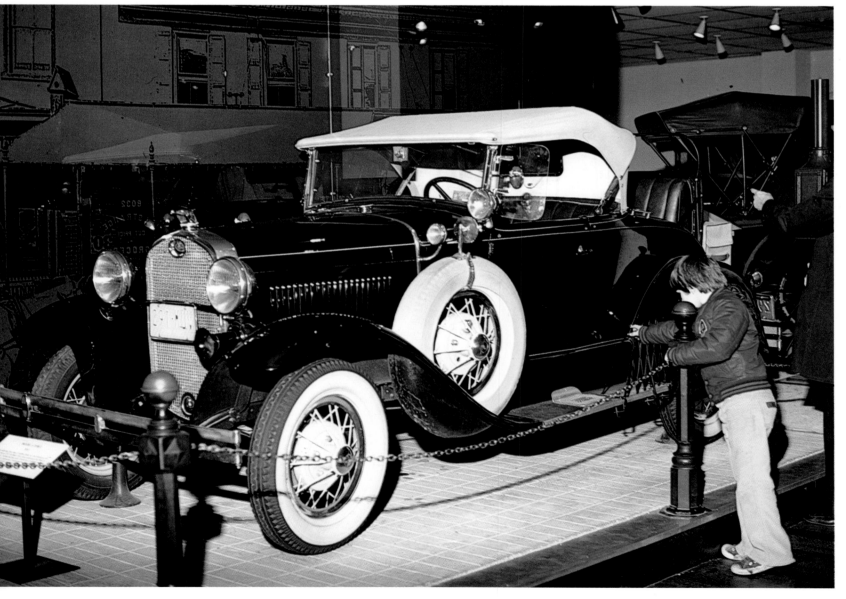

The Smithsonian National Gallery of Art (these pages) contains a wealth of paintings, sculpture and graphic art from both Europe and America which spans the centuries from the Middle Ages to the present day. Above: "The Maas at Dordrecht" by Dutch artist Aelbert Cuyp (c1620-1691) and (top center) "Apollo pursuing Daphne" by the Venetian Giovanni-Battista Tiepolo (1696-1770). Far right: "The White Girl" painted in 1862 by the American James Abbott McNeill Whistler, (top right) "Quadrille at the Moulin Rouge" by Toulouse-Lautrec (1864-1901) and (top) "Oarsman at Chatou" by Auguste Renoir (1841-1919). Right: "Children Playing on the Beach" by the American Mary Cassatt (1845-1926) and (center right) "Reclining Nude" by Raoul Dufy (1877-1953).

The inspiration, initial funding and core collection for the National Gallery of Art (these pages) came from Andrew Mellon, a Pittsburgh banker and philanthropist who, in 1936, offered to set up an American gallery along the lines of the National Gallery in London. Far right: "The Nymph of the Spring" by Lucas Cranach the Elder (1472-1553), (right) "Before the Ballet" by Hilaire-Germain-Edgar Degas (1834-1917) and (above far right) "Girl with a Watering Can" painted between 1872 and 1883 by Auguste Renoir. Above: "Self-Portrait", dated 1889, by Paul Gauguin (1848-1903) and (top) "Rouen Cathedral, West Facade, Sunlight" by Claude Monet (1840-1926). Above right: "The Lovers", painted in 1923 and belonging to Picasso's "neo-classical" period.

Top: the restored, 1899, Romanesque-Revival Old
Post Office, which now houses the Pavilion, a complex
of specialty shops, restaurants and food kiosks. Top
right: the Kennedy Center, (above) the Edgar Hoover
FBI Building and (right) the Supreme Court Building.
Facing page: Pershing Square.

Previous pages: the White House, originally designed by James Hoburn and begun in 1792, was barely habitable when its first presidential occupant, John Adams, arrived there in November 1800. Facing page: ornate ceilings and galleries in the Great Hall of the Library of Congress Building. The library began in 1800 as a one-room reference collection for Congress. In 1814 this was burned by the British, and was replaced by the fine private library of Thomas Jefferson. The main building, or Jefferson Building, an Italian Renaissance/Beaux-Arts creation modeled after the Paris Opera House, was built in 1897 and is now one of three housing a collection of millions of items which includes books, several thousand of them printed before 1500, photos, prints, sheet music and musical instruments. Below: old Union Station, now the National Visitor Center. The statue of General Andrew Jackson (left) in Lafayette Square, sculpted by Clark Mills in 1853, was the first equestrian statue cast in the US. The Iwo Jima Memorial (overleaf right bottom), sculpted by Felix W. de Weldon after Joe Rosenthal's Pulitzer Prize-winning photo, commemorates United States Marines who have died for their country. Overleaf left and right top: the United States Capitol.

The Navy Memorial Museum (these pages), in the Washington Navy Yard, presents an evocative display of famous ships, weapons and battle scenes from the last 200 years of American naval history.

Exhibits have been set up to give visitors, the young especially, a vivid experience: gun turrets move, periscopes are raised and lowered and battles re-enacted.

Work on Washington National Cathedral (above) began in 1893, when the Protestant Episcopal Cathedral Foundation was set up and Henry Yates Statterlee, the first Bishop of Washington, began acquiring land and raising funds. Building started in 1907 after two architects – Dr. George Bodley, a Briton, and the American Henry Vaughn – produced the initial design by dint of exchanging plans across the Atlantic, and in 1919 the architect Philip Frohman assumed control of the project. Faithfully designed in medieval Gothic style, the cathedral now stands imposingly on Mount Saint Alban Hill. Facing page: the Washington Monument, the world's tallest structure at its opening to the public in 1886.

Facing page: the Café Promenade. The Hay-Adams Hotel (top left and above right), the height of luxury among deluxe Washington hotels, is situated directly across from the White House and includes many dignitaries and heads of state on its guest list. Above left: a glittering chandelier in the elegant, 475-foot-long lobby of the Mayflower Hotel. Top right: the Gadsby Tavern.

All of America's paper money is printed at the Bureau of Engraving and Printing (above), together with invitations to the White House, treasury notes, military certificates and postage stamps. Tours provide the public with an insight into how their dollar bills are made and the inspiring spectacle of money rolling off the presses. Top: tulips and fountains near Union Station. Facing page: (top) the Thomas Jefferson Building of the Library of Congress, and (bottom) the Washington Monument.

Many of Washington's monuments and buildings of state are at their most spectacular at night, when floodlighting accentuates their balanced shapes against a background free from distraction. Top: Evan's 19-foot-high bronze statue of Jefferson circled by the marble pillars of the Jefferson Memorial and (above and facing page top) fountains and the dome of the United States Capitol. Facing page bottom: the futuristic outline of Dulles International Airport, Virginia, owned and operated by the Federal Government. Overleaf: the Lincoln Memorial, ghostly in winter twilight.

The building of Arlington House (right and facing page), overlooking what is now Arlington National Cemetery, was begun by George Washington Parke Custis, the adopted son of George and Martha Washington, in 1802. The Greek-Revival mansion was completed in 1820 and inherited by Custis' daughter, who married Lieutenant Robert E. Lee in 1831. Overrun when the Union Army crossed the Potomac during the Civil War, the mansion and land were seized by the federal government in 1864 for non-payment of dubiously-imposed taxes. When the house was finally returned to Lee's son in 1883 by a ruling of the Supreme Court, he sold it back to the government to be used as a national monument. Many of the original furnishings have been reassembled and the house restored as far as possible to its appearance when the home of the Robert E. Lees. Above: the 100-foot-high bell tower of the Robert A. Taft Memorial. Overleaf: the Air and Space Museum.

Pierre L'Enfant's intentions for Pennsylvania Avenue, that it should be "laid out on a dimension proportioned to the greatness which ... the Capital of a powerful Empire ought to manifest" apply equally to the whole of the city whose grand outlines he laid down. L'Enfant's plan worked on a large and balanced scale, and "The positions of the different Grand Edifices, and for the several Grand Squares ... were first determined on the most advantageous ground, commanding the most extensive prospects." Facing page: (top) the Lincoln Memorial and (bottom) the Arlington Memorial Amphitheater. Top: the Jefferson Memorial and (above) the prospect from the Capitol. Overleaf: tributes at the Vietnam Veterans Memorial.

NICK A AGUILAR Jr • CHARLES D ANNIS
EDWARD H ...ER • GARY L BROWN • BRIAN L BUSHNELL
...NEY • DAVI... ...ASLEY • DAVID P EVANS • PHILIP A HARRIS
...M JENERSO... ...HARD J KAUFFMAN • JOHN A KITRILAKIS
...RONE • JAM... ...MACE • JOHN B MULLIS • LEROY NELSON
...CK L W ...SK... ...CHARLES G SELMAN • WILLIAM H SMITH
...SKI • JAC... ...MMY CARRILLO • DANNY LEE DAWSON
...AS C M ...LEY • JAMES T HOWARD • DAVID C KAYS
...N POTT... ...IGHT A MASLINSKI • JOSEPH S NEMETH
...GALE... ...LES A PURSELL • RICHARD L WHITEMAN
...N C ... KEVIN A STOUT • EDWARD W STRAIN
...GARY ... ...O A DE LA GARZA Jr • HOWELL F BLAKEY
...O G R... ...AEL D CLICKNER • HARLAN E DANIELS
...RY V... ...M HELLMANN Jr • DANIEL C CASE
...N HO... ...RONNIE L JOHNSON • JAN H NELSON
...NIEL ... ...G RUYBAL • ROSENDO FLORES SILBAS
...D SU... ...GE H ADAMS • BRUCE E ARMSTRONG
...COOK ... ...AN D LANNES Jr • ROBERT F MERRILL
...RLOS H... ...S B ROBINSON • CHARLES N RUFFIN
...MES A H... ...LES R TOWNSEND • JAMES F AUSTIN
...AWFORD • CLIFFORD J EARNHARDT
...GARCIA-GARAY • BENNY D GREENE
...SLAW KAUS • THOMAS J LAUGHLIN
W 12

MELVIN BOWMAN • MIC...
GREGORY A CHA...
JON H DOOLITTLE • SY...
BRUCE E HAHN • PHILLIP R HA...
TOMMY I HINDMAN ...
JESSE GOMEZ JUAREZ • ALBE...
FRANK F LEWIS ...
GARY R KIESELBURG • MICKEY ...
ROY C RANSOM • ...
RONALD D VAN BEUKERING ...
JOHN G WIDEN • ...
WILLIE D ARMS • PAUL ALIPIO B...
WAYNE R BEBO...
PETER A COOK • JOHN E DA...
RONALD E FITZGERALD ...
THOMAS E HASLET • LAWRENC...
KENNETH B KENDALL • ...
NEAL A LORD Jr • ...
RAYMOND D MARECK • WILLIA...
GARY P RADER • JOSEP...
JOHN L WILSON • BERNA...
SHELBY M CARTE...
LARRY A FOSTER ...
• CLIFFORD E JE...

Above: peaceful evening light on the Potomac River and (facing page) the Reflecting Pool. Overleaf: the red brick and charm of residential Washington backed by the great white buildings of the formal city. East Capitol Street leads up past the Supreme Court on the right and the Library of Congress on the left to the United States Capitol, from which L'Enfant's true line "due East and West" continues as the Mall to the Washington Monument.

Facing page: striking examples of the variety of styles present in Washington's architecture. (Top left) the Capitol, (top right) the East Building of the National Gallery of Art, (bottom left) the Supreme Court building and (bottom right) the Smithsonian Institution Building. Above: the Jefferson Drive entrance to the National Air and Space Museum. The terraced Hirshhorn Sculpture Garden (overleaf), sunken six to fourteen feet below the level of the Mall, provides a serene setting in which to view fine sculpture.

Spring flowers, (facing page top) below the Bureau of Engraving and Printing, (above) on Pennsylvania Avenue and (facing page bottom and top) lighting the shore of the Potomac River in Lady Bird Johnson Park. Overleaf: evening light (left) on the Jefferson Memorial and (right) illuminating the Lincoln Memorial, the Washington Monument and the United States Capitol.

The fine buildings and ordered gardens of Washington today were once a very distant dream and one which seemed to many unattainable. When George Washington fixed upon the location for the new capital it was little more than an almost flat tract of woodland and marshy ground, and, due partly to lack of funds, it was for many years "neither town nor village," described by the Irish poet Thomas Moore as "This embryo capital, where Fancy sees squares in morasses, obelisks in trees." Facing page: (top) the Reflecting Pool seen from the steps of the Lincoln Memorial, and (bottom and above) sculpture and tulips outside the National Museum of American History. Left: the Jefferson Drive entrance to the National Air and Space Museum.

The National Zoological Park (this page) was established in 1890 under the direction of the Smithsonian Institution, and moved its pens from the Mall to its present site at Rock Creek largely to provide suitable facilities to preserve the American Bison from extinction. Today, the zoo covers 176 acres and its charges include many rare and endangered species. Top left: totem pcle marking the blue Polar Bear Trail and (above left) the Great Flight Cage. Facing page: (top) the Hirshhorn Sculpture Garden and (bottom) a mass of color in the National Arboretum.

The US Botanic Gardens, at the foot of Capitol Hill, consists mainly of a cast iron and glass Victorian-style conservatory (these pages), built in 1902. Here flourishes a permanent collection of tropical, sub-tropical and desert plants, including many varieties of orchids (facing page bottom), such as *Cattleya Trianae* (above left), Phar Edelweiss (top center), Paph Hailoa (above), and Barbara Billingsly and Margaret Stuart (below left). Cacti (left) and poinsettias (facing page top) also occupy sections of the conservatory. Overleaf: a stately colonnade of trees near the Washington Monument.

Below: the Church Triumphant, the south rose window, and (facing page) the west Creation Rose window, in Washington National Cathedral (these pages). Bottom left: the Theology of Baptism window and (bottom) the Scientists and Technicians (Space) window, its colors inspired by photographs taken during space travel.

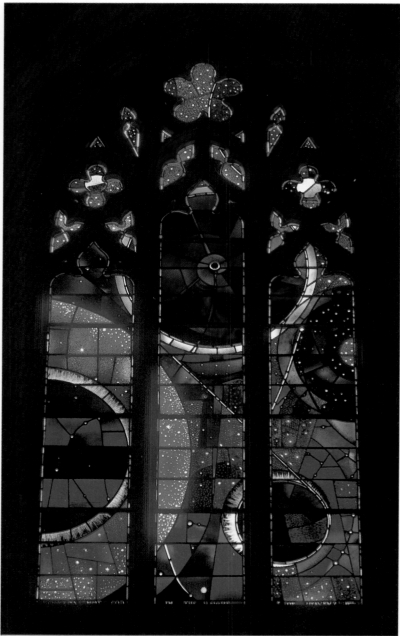

Previous pages: examples of Victorian ingenuity, part of the collection of American Victoriana on show at the Arts and Industries Building. Facing page: (top) Ionic columns of the Jefferson Memorial and (bottom) Rodin's "Burghers of Calais" in the Hirshhorn Sculpture Garden. Top: cherries in bloom along the Mall and (above) tulips around the Navy Marine Memorial. Overleaf: (left bottom) the Tomb of the Unknowns and (remaining pictures) Mount Vernon. At the height of its prosperity under the ownership and running of George Washington, the Mount Vernon estate covered 8,000 acres divided into five working farms.

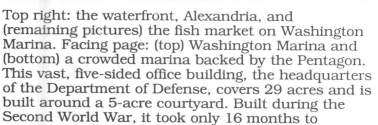

Top right: the waterfront, Alexandria, and (remaining pictures) the fish market on Washington Marina. Facing page: (top) Washington Marina and (bottom) a crowded marina backed by the Pentagon. This vast, five-sided office building, the headquarters of the Department of Defense, covers 29 acres and is built around a 5-acre courtyard. Built during the Second World War, it took only 16 months to

complete. The Iwo Jima Memorial (overleaf), depicting the moment, captured on film by Joe Rosenthal, when five marines and a sailor raised the American flag on Mount Suribachi during the Second World War, is among Washington's most poignant commemorations of those who have given their lives for the nation.